A WINDOW TO THE
SOUTHERN HIGHLANDS

AUTHOR
Linda Emery

EDITOR
Sandra Denholm

DESIGNER
Judy Echin

A HIGHLIFE PUBLICATION

ACKNOWLEDGMENTS

PHOTOGRAPHERS

Tony Sheffield

Bob Hughes

John Payne

Jackie Ranken

Brett Gregory

Tom Dimec

Leonie Knapman

Kathie Atkinson

Max Wilson

Thomas Petrie

Richard Cant

Tim Mooney

Lorna Rose

Lynn McColl

SPECIAL THANKS TO

Berrima District Historical Society

Tourism Southern Highlands

National Parks and Wildlife Service

Published by Canongate Partners Pty Ltd, publishers of HIGHLife Magazine, 443 Moss Vale Road, Bowral NSW 2576 ABN 41 231 971 675

ISBN 0 9578942 0 1

CONTENTS

INTRODUCTION

We came into a most beautiful country, being nothing but fine
large meadows with ponds of water in them, fine green hills but very thin
of timber ... in my opinion one of the finest in the known world.
It certainly must be a pleasure to any man to view so fine a country.

From the top of Mt Gingenbullen at Sutton Forest, this is the description of the Southern Highlands written in 1798 by a young man in the first European exploration party to pass through the area. Two centuries later, while so much has changed, the Southern Highlands is still a most beautiful country. The people who live here feel a strong sense of place and an awareness of the beauty that everywhere surrounds them. And there is a community pride in knowing that so many others from all over Australia – and beyond – share their sentiments.

The Southern Highlands attracts over a million visitors each year who come to enjoy Highland style – wonderful shopping, fine restaurants and cafes, spectacular scenery and a rich history. There is something for everyone, from the simple pleasure of a drive through the countryside to a weekend of indulgence at one of the luxury resorts. For lovers of the great outdoors, the district boasts six golf courses within a 10 kilometre radius, outstanding equestrian facilities, horse riding, polo and polocrosse and fly fishing in the numerous rivers, creeks and dams. In the national parks and bushland reserves are walking tracks from the short and easy to those that challenge the most serious bushwalker.

The Highlands is home to a large community of painters, artisans and craftspeople and their work, fine art and quality prints, unique contemporary furniture and glass can be found in the numerous art and craft galleries. Antique shops abound, dealing in items of rare quality and every imaginable collectable and each weekend there are markets in one of the towns or villages, where quirky craft, plants, home baking and fresh local produce beg to be taken home. Visitors can choose to stay in a stylish cottage, a cosy bed and breakfast, a grand country house, a modern resort – or merely bring their own tent.

Much of the appeal of the Highlands is the climate, where the four seasons are so much more sharply defined than on the coastal plains. Winters are cool with average temperatures ranging from zero to 12 degrees and in summer from 12 to 28 degrees. Spring and autumn are the sensational seasons, when the days are warm and the air clear and fresh. As summer fades, the exotic trees that so characterise the district shed their brilliant autumn leaves before the winter sleep and in spring the gardens that have made the area so famous burst into bloom.

A geologically distinct area, the Southern Highlands is an undulating high plateau averaging 700 metres above sea level and isolated from surrounding areas by steep escarpments, deep gorges and rocky infertile forests. The abundantly endowed Highland landscape is separated from the coastal plains to the east by the Illawarra Escarpment and in the west by the rugged terrain of the valleys of the Wingecarribee and Wollondilly Rivers. The mighty Shoalhaven River formed the sheer cliffs and gorges that signal the southern end of the plateau and in the north, the Nepean River system similarly marks the divide between the poor sandy soils of the Hawkesbury sandstone belt and the rich volcanic soils of the beautiful green island that is the Southern Highlands.

The processes that produced this green and pleasant land began 55 million years ago when huge lava flows spilled out of the active volcanoes of Mt Gibraltar and Mt Jellore. Most of the soil on the Highland plateau is derived from Wianamatta Shales, with the pockets of rich, red basalt soils that occur around Exeter, Kangaloon and Robertson coming from the weathered, ancient lava.

Today, some 41,000 people live in the Wingecarribee Shire over an area of 2700 square kilometres. Although separated by just 15 kilometres, the three main towns of the Southern Highlands – Mittagong, Bowral and Moss Vale – have their own distinctive characters. The majority of the population lives within the rough triangle they form, but scattered throughout the rest of the shire are some 20 villages that range from a tiny cluster of houses or an old church and graveyard, to rapidly growing residential areas. Each is different, has its own story to tell and a charm of its own.

This book is a window to the Southern Highlands. It is an expression of the themes that define the character of the area – its history, farming in all its forms, the architecture and gardens. In seeking to explore these themes, we need to look to the past, for it defines our present and the present our future. But the past is not another country and this is perhaps no better illustrated than in the Southern Highlands, for the qualities that are most admired in the area today are the result of the directions taken well over a century ago. A salutary lesson, for there is no doubt that the Highlands is unique in many ways and if its environmental and cultural values are to be preserved, we, the present custodians, must set a firm direction for the future.

LINDA EMERY

BOWRAL
& DISTRICT

BOWRAL
& DISTRICT

Bowral, with its stylish boutiques, cafes and restaurants is the hub of the Southern Highlands. Few places in New South Wales command such a fine reputation, established long ago, as a rural retreat, a place to escape the city and the heat and humidity of the coastal plain. Bowral is like a bridge between town and country, exuding the charm of a solid and prosperous rural town with an element of city chic. Its attractive tree-lined streets, outstanding gardens and the beauty of its location, nestled within in the protective arms of Mt. Gibraltar and Oxley's Hill continue to draw visitors and increasingly, new residents.

But Bowral's present is inseparable from its past. From the time it became known as "The Sanitorium of the South" in the late 1880s, the town attracted people who could afford a country house and garden and the staff to maintain them. The legacy of the development that took place over a century ago is the look that Bowral has today – leafy, substantial, elegant.

European settlement in the area goes back to 1816, when explorer and Surveyor General of NSW, Lieutenant John Oxley, sent his stockmen and cattle to graze a run he called Wingecarribee. It became the southern outpost of his main property at Kirkham, near Camden. Eventually receiving grants of some 4200 acres in the area, John Oxley's sons subdivided a portion of their Wingecarribee Estate into town lots in 1858 and so Bowral, the name used by the local Aboriginal people, the Gundungurra, for the mountain we know as Mt. Gibraltar, was born.

John Norton Oxley chose the street names, also of Aboriginal origin – Merrigang Street for the native dog that inhabited the hills of the Mittagong Range, Banyette for a local Aboriginal girl, Boolwey for a property on the Berrima Road. Wingecarribee Street led to the Oxley home and Bong Bong Street to the village of Bong Bong on the Wingecarribee River, the site of the first European settlement in the Southern Highlands.

Until the rail line from Sydney to Moss Vale opened in 1867, growth was slow, but by the 1870s, the ease of travel made possible by trains and the concept of leisure time and holidays for a growing middle class

A Window To The Southern Highlands

*The town of
Bowral from above
Mt Gibraltar*

came together and Bowral's future direction was set.

The country estates that grew up in the late 19th and early 20th centuries in and around Bowral contributed to the town's fame as a place of magnificent gardens. Today, some of the finest private gardens in NSW are to be found in the Bowral area, not only the well-known at *Milton Park* and *Kennerton Green*, but many new gardens that cover a range of styles from rambling cottage gardens to formal Tuscan elegance.

Outstanding examples of rare and exotic trees can be seen in full maturity in the grounds of the refined "gentleman's residences" built in Burradoo for some of Sydney's leading families more than a century ago. Even though most of these properties have shrunk in size through subdivision, the old and new blend comfortably and Burradoo remains a residential area of great charm and style. Indeed, many recently built homes in the leafy enclave of Burradoo are set to become the classic country houses of the future.

But Bowral is more than its climate and gardens. On a different level, there is a tradition of cultural awareness and a rich history of literary, educational and artistic life in the town. Many authors, musicians, artists and academics have been drawn to Bowral, among them P.L. Travers, famous as the author of

Tulip Time in Corbett Gardens and (opposite) the rectory of St Simon and St Jude's

Mary Poppins, and Arthur Upfield, creator of Boney, the eponymously named detective novels, which later became the basis of a television series.

Tourism has always been central to the economy of Bowral and the town boasts some of the finest tourist facilities to be found anywhere, from luxurious country resorts and hotels to secluded cottage hideaways. The climate influences the character and style of accommodation and the appeal of comfortable armchairs in front of a crackling open fire, snuggly feather doonas and colourful cottage gardens is irresistible to many a city visitor. In the trendy boutiques and retail stores visitors can shop in a relaxed and friendly atmosphere for everything from designer clothing, homewares and exclusive gifts to antiques, artworks and books.

And when it's time to eat, the selection is just as varied. Cafe society is part and parcel of Bowral life and as well as bistros serving the best in contemporary and innovative Australian food, you can try Italian, Thai, Indian or Chinese restaurants.

Corbett Gardens is the delightful town park that for three weeks in September and October is the focus of the Tulip Time festival in Bowral. Thousands of tulips and other spring flowering bulbs are planted in the gardens and the vibrant displays in this public park and the many private gardens that open their gates for charity attract crowds of visitors to the Southern Highlands. But for the rest of the year it is a quiet haven where, without the riot of spring colour, the mature rhododendrons, azaleas, conifers and towering oak trees can be appreciated for their own worth. The view from Corbett Gardens down Bendooley Street takes in one of the key historic precincts of Bowral, a streetscape that retains its 19th century character. Right along the eastern side of Bendooley Street, from the Bowral Court House to St Simon and St Jude's Anglican Church is an unbroken line of well preserved public buildings. The unusual design of the Court House, completed in 1895 using trachyte from the Bowral Quarries on the Gib, sits happily next to the

A precinct of historic buildings in Bendooley Street ... Bowral School of Arts completed in 1885
as a single storey building with the top storey added in 1913 and the Town Hall built in 1889

Bong Bong Street, Bowral, in 1940. In the foreground is the war memorial and park, left is the CBC building demolished in the 1970s, and at the right, the Royal Hotel which has just regained its original name after refurbishment

An old weatherboard cottage, now a restaurant, in Boolwey Street and Harvest Festival in Bowral

A charming wooden bridge over Mittagong Creek, Shepherd Street, Bowral

more predictable former Council Chambers and School of Arts, built in the more exuberant style of the 1880s. On the next corner, St Jude's Rectory is one of the most significant Victorian buildings in Bowral. Completed in 1880, this charming house is set amidst a typical Bowral garden of exotic trees, roses and cottage perennials. And opposite the church is Bowral Public School attended by a young Don Bradman, Bowral's most famous son.

The Bowral of the past perhaps had an image of an older, more conservative population and retirement has certainly been the catalyst for many people to make the move to Bowral. Demographically, the Southern Highlands is a little different from the rest of NSW. There are significantly more over 55s than the State average and a large number of self-funded retirees. They bring to the district a wealth of knowledge and wisdom which is channelled into a myriad community, sporting and self-help activities. At the other end of the scale, children under 15 make up a greater proportion of the population than in many other areas of the State.

In recent years, there has been something of a shift and new developments have resulted in an increase in the number of younger people moving into the area. Many seek an escape from city living; for others the prospect of an affordable home is the attraction. Productive dairying and cattle grazing properties are now more valuable as residential land and so, on the periphery of the town, the once rolling green hills have been replaced by suburban housing estates.

Careful planning will secure the future of Bowral and the characteristics that have so long drawn people to it. At a local government level, there is a will to retain some of the planning philosophy of the past that has kept the town relatively free from heavy industry while looking at innovative ways to implement sustainable development.

As it was from its very beginnings, Bowral is a town confident of its place in the world. The future envisaged by the early residents seems to be mirrored in the

rapid population growth that has taken place in recent years. Bowral has so far managed to retain its appeal both as a place to live and as a rural retreat and as the city draws ever closer to the country, let it always remain so.

Shepherd Street Bowral and (left) Kilbirnie House in Burradoo

A 1930s view of Milton Park and (right) in its mature garden

There could be no more appropriate location for a public museum specialising in cricket than in the town where Sir Donald Bradman grew up and learned to play the game. And there could surely be no more picturesque setting than the beautiful Glebe Park and Bradman Oval where cricket has been played for more than a century.

Don Bradman came with his family to Bowral in 1911 at the age of two, but their relationship with the district went back much further, to when his grandparents married in Berrima in 1860. Much of The Don's early cricket was played on the oval opposite the family home in Glebe Street. Named the Bradman Oval in 1947, the pitch has been significantly improved by the Bradman Museum Trust in recent years and the addition of the white picket fence around the boundary makes this the quintessential country cricket ground.

With the support of Sir Donald, the first stage of the museum project became a reality in 1989, when he and Lady Bradman attended the opening of the pavilion. This charming building served as a temporary exhibition space during the planning and construction of the museum proper, which was opened on August 27, 1996, Sir Donald's 88th birthday.

The Bradman Museum now houses one of the best collections of cricketing memorabilia in the world, including many items from Sir Donald's personal collection. But it is more than a place for students of the history of cricket and lovers of the game. The exhibitions convey the sense of what cricket has meant to generations of Australians and the part it played in their everyday lives. Whether they played on a dusty pitch in the country, the fine turf wickets of the great cricket grounds, or just chased balls around the backyard for big brothers who never got out, all visitors are fascinated by the story the museum tells.

The view from
Minnows Drive

Horse stalls at the 1903 races and (opposite) a drystone wall

Bong Bong Picnic Race Day is a much-anticipated event on the Southern Highlands social calendar. In November each year, the picturesque Wyeera course on Kangaloon Road just a few kilometres from Bowral, comes alive as horses and riders, punters and bookmakers, spectators and picnickers set up for a day of fun and fashion. Tempestuous spring weather in the Highlands can range from perfect sunshine to howling gales, but nothing dampens the spirits of picnic racegoers. This is the day to wear elegant and outrageous hats, fashions to equal the best at Sydney and Melbourne racing carnivals, and to enjoy fine food and wine.

First staged in 1887, for their first 15 years the races were held at "Throsby Park", Moss Vale, on what was long known as Racecourse Paddock. In those days club members represented a Who's Who of society in the Highlands and Goulburn. In its heyday, the race meeting was held over two days and was often attended by the NSW governor if he happened to be at his official country residence, Hillview at Sutton Forest.

Breathlessly reported in the local press, with wonderful descriptions of the ladies' gowns, the Bong Bong Race Ball was a glamorous affair. More than a century after the excitement of the first race day, the present day incarnation of the Bong Bong Races continues the traditions of the past.

*A*sk someone to name the things they most associate with the Southern Highlands and almost certainly mention will be made of Bradman and they may well speak of bulbs. But books? Not yet, but if the booksellers of the Highlands have their way, that is precisely what will happen.

Bowral has recently become the first town in Australia to become part of the international Booktown movement that began almost 40 years ago in Hay-on-Wye, a small town on the border of England and Wales. Richard Booth, an eccentric bookseller, had a grand plan – to have the biggest bookshop in the world. As his shop grew, so did the number of visitors who came to the town and gradually, the number of booksellers, until Hay-on-Wye became known as "The Booktown". For booklovers, the appeal of taking a trip to the countryside to a town where they could browse in some 30 bookshops was tantamount to paradise.

So successful has the concept become that there are now some 20 similar ventures in various parts of the world. Bowral has all the credentials for a Booktown, located as it is close to the major population centres of NSW and in a scenic rural area with an existing tourist infrastructure. Australians already have a high per capita rate of book buying and in Bowral the exposure to bookshops is even greater than that of the country as a whole. The district is well served by a range of interesting and well-known booksellers, including Messrs Berkelouw, (pictured left) a firm that has been in the business of selling fine and rare books for six generations.

Some 17 Southern Highlands bookshops and related enterprises have joined together to promote Australia's first Booktown and to foster the love of books and reading. Unlike Hay-on-Wye and other cities and towns throughout the world, these booksellers are not concentrated in one place, but in towns and villages throughout the Highlands. So the booksellers have used the name "Booktrail" rather than "Booktown". As it is poised to become a mecca for booklovers and collectors from all over Australia, the Highlands should soon be known for the three B's ... Bradman, bulbs – and books.

Vineyards near Centennial Road

The old tanning shed on the outskirts of Bowral, a wonderful example of rural heritage and (above) Kirkland Road

Kangaloon in the snow

Misty morning near Bowral

*Bowral in a
sea of mist*

Nestled into the side of Oxley's Hill and overlooking the town of Bowral is "Wingecarribbee", built in 1857 by the son of explorer John Oxley. Henry Molesworth Oxley ordered the house in 1854 from the catalogue of Samuel Hemming's foundry in Bristol, England, and had it shipped to NSW. A rare example of a 19th century prefabricated iron house, it literally arrived in Sydney in boxes. This original "kit home" was complete in every way, from the timber for framing, doors, windows and shutters, the heavy galvanised corrugated iron for the roof and walls and the iron screws and bolts that kept it all together. Components were numbered which, according to the plan, would make assembly of the house easy. As well as the building materials, the kit included interior fixtures and furnishings, even curtains of Nottingham lace that still hang in the drawing room. The furniture in this room includes a French ship's piano with folding keyboard and ornate candle sconces. An apothecary chest that belonged to John Oxley sits atop the piano. Three generations of Oxleys lived in the house before it passed to the present owners, related through marriage to the family.

Oxley's Hill Road between Bowral and Berrima

A winter's morning on Range Road

Tree plantation near Bowral and (above)
a stark trunk on Old South Road

Old South Road, Bowral and (right) stock crossing
over the Wingecarribee River at Burradoo

*Wingecarribee
Reservoir from
above Kangaloon
Road*

Farmhouse at Kangaloon

Left: Oxley's Hill Road and (right) Kangaloon village hall

MOSS VALE

& DISTRICT

MOSS VALE
& DISTRICT

Moss Vale and Bowral are separated by just 10 kilometres and a small river, the Wingecarribee, but in many respects the towns are poles apart. Still very much a country town, Moss Vale is the rural heart of the Highlands and the service centre for the best productive rural properties in the area. Bowral may have the trendiest shopping streets, but if you want to buy and sell livestock, Moss Vale is the place to go.

As the headquarters of the Wingecarribee Shire Council, the town is the civic centre of the area. Amalgamated from three separate council bodies in 1981, Wingecarribee Shire covers an area of 2700 square kilometres and with only 41,000 residents, that ratio has considerable implications in terms of provi-

sion of services. With 320 staff, as well as a number of private contractors, the council is the biggest single employer in the Southern Highlands which in itself brings certain advantages to Moss Vale.

The town and the Highlands in general derive great economic benefit from a significant industrial sector located in the Moss Vale/Berrima corridor. But with tourism the main income producer for the Highlands, the long-term strategy for the Wingecarribee Shire is to ensure that future development will not compromise the attributes that continue to attract visitors to the area. "Clean and green" are the buzzwords for future industrial development in Moss Vale.

Today, Bowral is the largest and fastest growing of

An aerial view of Moss Vale looking east and (previous page) looking north east to Moss Vale from Oldbury Road

the three main Highlands towns, but it wasn't always so and for many years Moss Vale outstripped its northern sister both in population and commercial activity. Named for Jemmy Moss, an ex-convict who worked for local landowner Charles Throsby, Moss Vale began in 1863 as a small sub-division of Throsby land around the new Great Southern Railway. Other local landowners soon followed suit and by the time the station opened in 1867, the town had a store, postal service and hotel, mainly to cater for the needs of the large number of railway workers and their families who had come to the district. Their small tent communities sprang up all along the railway line as it forged south towards Goulburn.

By the late 1870s, Moss Vale was experiencing the first influences of tourism and was showing all the signs of a town on the move. During the 1860s the opening up of the Yarrawa Brush, the area around Robertson, Burra-wang and Wildes Meadow, added to the importance of the rail head at Moss Vale, which became the district centre for sending produce, livestock and other freight to the Sydney market.

As the rural hub of the district, in March each year the town stages that well-known feature of country life, the Agricultural Show. Since 1884 when the first show was held on 10 acres of land leased from the Throsby family, this annual event has grown into a

Art and antique shops in Moss Vale

local institution. For the equestrian set and cattle breeders, it is one of the important lead-up shows to the Sydney Royal Easter Show.

Not far south of Moss Vale is Sutton Forest where some of the best of the district's properties were developed from land grants made in the 1820s. Small as it is today, the outward impression of this delightful village belies the important part it played in the early history of white settlement in the Southern Highlands. Well maintained historic buildings, carefully tended roadside tree plantings and the many flags flying from poles around this small hamlet show the great pride the residents have in their village and its past.

The earliest contact Europeans had with the area was in 1798 when a small exploration party climbed nearby Mt. Gingenbullen. Surveying the scene before them, they waxed lyrical about its beauty, but it was to be another 20 years before the first settlers in the district took up small acreages and began to build their community. In those early days of settlement, Sutton Forest was a generic term used to describe all the area we know today as the Southern Highlands, with the village as its social centre.

Sutton Forest's first public building was All Saints Chapel and burial ground, begun in 1828 and now the oldest and most interesting of the many historic churchyards in the Southern Highlands. Here the pioneer settlers, both humble and exalted, mix on equal terms, their epitaphs reaching down through the years to tell the stories of times past. The present sandstone church was built in 1861, replacing a little wooden chapel that once served settlers as far south as Yass and the Monaro. A number of small inns, both legal and illegal, sprang up in Sutton Forest from the early 1830s, followed by the usual general stores, butcher and baker, post and telegraph office and in 1879, the public school, still going strong after 120 years. On the hill overlooking the village is *Hillview*, the former vice-regal residence that bestowed such cachet on the little town as a succession of NSW governors came to stay. Some of the finest country houses in the Highlands,

Cattle, Yarrawa Road, Moss Vale and (right) Iona Park Road

many built in the late 19th century for wealthy Sydney families are dotted in and around Sutton Forest. Another village landmark known to many travellers was The Everything Store that sold, well ... everything! Bursting at the seams with the most amazing array of items, the shop, as well as being the local general store, was a magnet for bargain hunters from far and wide and the subject of innumerable paintings, drawings and photographs. The Everything Store and its alter ego across the road, A Little Piece of Scotland, are still owned by the same family, but instead of the floor to ceiling clutter of yesteryear they have now gone considerably upmarket and continue to draw visitors to the village.

Sutton Forest also marks the start of one of the prettiest tourist drives in the Southern Highlands. The Highland Way winds through a landscape of rich pastures and tall stands of native and exotic trees, small cottage gardens and gardens of grand proportions until it reaches the quaint village of Exeter. First settled by

Oldbury, Sutton Forest, built c1828 by James Atkinson

the Badgery family in the 1820s, the township was named for their English city of origin. Tall oaks, elms and poplars arch majestically over the road and around the charming Exeter Park that looks so like an English village green – no more so than in November each year when the Exeter Village Fayre brings the oval to life. Morris dancers, fair damsels, Cavaliers and

Moss Vale cottage

Roundheads mix with thousands of visitors enjoying everything from mediaeval banquets and pork pies to real ale from the English pub that is set up especially for the day. Set amidst beautifully landscaped grounds opposite the park, St Aidan's Anglican Church was built in 1895 from local basalt stone. Named for the Irish monk Aidan, who journeyed from Iona to Lindisfarne to bring Christianity to Northern England in 635AD, the church has a distinctly Celtic look and, surmounted by the traditional cross of St Aidan, is like no other church in the Southern Highlands. The many large exotic trees that surround the church are a legacy of its early days when Arthur Yates of the seed-growing firm was a regular parishioner and did much

to help beautify the church grounds and the village of Exeter.

Both Arthur Yates & Co and Searl Bros, the other leading seed and bulb grower in the early 20th century, had commercial farms in Exeter. The rich volcanic soil and cool climate made it ideal for horticulture and in spring, the daffodil farm at Searl's would send thousands of flowers by rail to the markets in Sydney. Today the farms have gone, but the trees and gardens that were planted so long ago live on, exemplifying the character of Exeter so admired by residents and visitors alike. *Invergowrie*, the former Yates property, has one of the most splendid gardens in Exeter. Using the mature trees planted by Arthur Yates as a framework, landscape gardener Paul Sorensen planned the present garden in the 1930s for its new owners, Sir Cecil and Lady (Dorothy) Hoskins. Magnificent rhododendrons are but one feature of the garden that became deservedly famous as a fine example of the English landscape style.

At the end of the Highland Way and at the southernmost reach of the Wingecarribee Shire is Bundanoon – "a place of big deep gullies". So the Gundungurra people, the first inhabitants, named this spectacular area perched on the edge of the Illawarra Escarpment. With the great natural beauty of the Morton National Park literally at their back door, the 3000 residents of Bundanoon consider themselves fortunate to live in such a special place.

The growth of Bundanoon in its early days, like so many of the Highlands towns and villages, rested heavily on the development of the area as a holiday destination. From the late 1880s guest houses began to spring up to cater for the mostly city visitors who came to indulge the Victorian passion for picnics, bushwalking and generally communing with nature. Bundanoon Gullies Reserve was created to give them the opportunity to experience the great scenic beauty, flora and fauna of the area. Much of the early work of forming tracks, cutting steps and making lookouts in the reserve was done by local volunteers, a tradition that

Tree-lined entrance to a property on Golden Vale Road

continues today with an active local group, The Friends of Morton Park, helping maintain and conserve this precious natural environment.

In its heyday between the wars, Bundanoon was the tourist mecca of the Highlands. More than 60 guest houses operated at one time or another, from a few rooms in family homes to those that catered for up to 130 guests. Several of these had their own golf courses and tennis courts. At night, dances were held in the larger establishments and films shown in the hall when the "picture show man" came to town. One of the busiest periods in Bundanoon was during World War II when the threat of invasion seemed very real. Hundreds of people left Sydney with their children for the perceived safety of the country. Guest houses were full to overflowing and the reality of war seemed a very long way away as the evacuees enjoyed all the activities and entertainment the village had to offer.

By the 1950s, a decline in tourist towns like Bundanoon had begun. The post-war boom provided people with the financial means to travel further afield, many in their own cars, once a luxury limited to a privileged few. One by one, the accommodation houses closed, but today, the wheel seems to have turned full circle. After a long sleep, guest houses are enjoying a resurgence in popularity and Bundanoon now offers a range of accommodation from the cosy youth hostel to luxury accommodation in beautifully restored homes.

While tourism is still an important contributor to the Bundanoon economy, in recent years the town has developed as a peaceful and desirable residential area. The village has so far retained the feel of a small Australian town of years gone by, something that the local community association works hard to foster.

Moss Vale and the southern villages are bound together through their history and rural heritage. To some degree they are on the path less trod but this only adds to the charm, for it is the fact that they have retained many of the qualities of bygone days that make them distinct from other parts of the Southern Highlands.

Moss Vale Golf Course and Dormie House

Horbury Hunt designed Hamilton House became Tudor House school in 1902

Christ Church Bong Bong at Moss Vale (1845), the oldest church in the Southern Highlands

Gum trees swathed in gold on Oldbury Road
and tangled trees on Berrima Road

A Little Piece of Scotland, Sutton Forest, specialises in all things Scottish

The Everything Store at Sutton Forest continues to draw visitors to the village

Riders at Danric Lodge, Sutton Forest

Early footstone in the churchyard of All Saints, Sutton Forest

All Saints Church and churchyard, Sutton Forest

Undulating hills along Canyonleigh Road

The grounds of Hillview, former country residence of NSW governors

Berrima Horse Trials, Sutton Forest

*S*tepping on to the platform of the quaint Hornby-like railway station at Exeter is like stepping back in time. Opened in 1878 as Badgery's Siding, it was renamed Exeter in 1890 when the Badgery family's "Vine Lodge" property through which it passed was subdivided. As the village developed, Exeter became the busiest of the small stations in the district handling transport to the Sydney markets for the livestock, milk, fruit, vegetables and flowers from the local farms. Exeter is well known among railway aficionados for its unique character. The manually operated signal box and signalling system are still in use, rare surviving examples of late 19th century technologies. Indeed, the few kilometres of track between Exeter and Bundanoon are the only section of the Main Southern Railway Line that has not been automated. At an elevation of 717 metres, the station at Exeter (village pictured left) is the highest on the Sydney-Melbourne line.

Halcyon, an early weatherboard cottage in Exeter once used as the post office

Antique shop in Exeter, formerly Moorecroft and Akrigg's General Store

Exeter General Store and St Aidan's Church

Monks at the Sunnataram Buddhist Monastery, Bundanoon

On the road to Wingello

Bundanoon is home to one of the largest and most successful highland gatherings in Australia. Each April, the town is magically transformed for a day into the mythical village of Brigadoon and some 20,000 people swell the population of this normally quiet town. From the moment the sounds of a lone piper are heard at dawn, the day is a celebration of all things Scottish. Kilts are de rigueur, particularly since a new district tartan was designed and registered. The colours were chosen to represent the motifs of Bundanoon – green for the gullies, yellow for the wattle, white for the mist that so often rolls in to blanket the town and blue for the sky when it doesn't!

More than 20 pipe bands from all over NSW gather for the street parade and massed band displays on the oval. Highland and Scottish country dancers perform everything from the Highland Fling and sword dance to reels and strathspeys, accompanied by some of Australia's finest exponents of Scottish fiddle music. Traditional contests such as the tossing of the caber, the kilted dash, the hammer throw and haggis hurling are keenly fought.

The most anticipated competition of the day is the lifting of the Stones of Manhood. In Scottish history, a boy was considered to have reached manhood when he could lift two stones in weight from the ground on to the top of a stone wall, a tradition that is said to be more than 1000 years old. Revived in Scotland in the 1970s, the contest has now become just as popular in Australia. Competitors must lift a set of five round stones, ranging in weight from 100 to 150 kg, from the ground on to the top of large wooden barrels. Quarried and manufactured at the local quarry seven years ago, the Bundanoon Stones have a reputation among "strong men" the world over.

Once the Pill Factory built in 1896 by local entrepreneur W. A. (Gus) Nicholas as a factory for his homeopathic cure-all powders and pills, now a motel. Right: Bundanoon shops

Exeter in the mist

Golden Vale Road, Sutton Forest, at dusk

The rich farmlands
of Robertson

*Nowra Road, Moss Vale and (below) Sheepwash
Road, Moss Vale. Right: Wildes Meadow*

*Burrawang
from the air with
Fitzroy Falls
Reservoir in the
distance*

Fitzroy Falls forms the northern boundary of the wild and beautiful Morton National Park. Countless thousands of visitors have thrilled to the sight and sound of the waters of Yarrunga Creek as they plunge over the clifftop to the valley floor about 100 metres below. Named for Governor Sir Charles FitzRoy when he visited this already well-known beauty spot in 1850, the falls have been a tourist drawcard ever since.

Now covering an area of some 1900 square kilometres, Morton National Park is one of the largest parks in Australia. From a leisurely clifftop walk to view the falls to a more challenging trek into the valley, the park offers recreational opportunities for everyone. The environmentally-friendly Fitzroy Falls Visitor Centre is designed to blend into its surroundings using local sandstone and huge beams recycled from the original timber bridge over Yarrunga Creek. The centre operates an educational facility on the flora and fauna of the region. Boardwalks direct visitors under the road and through the bush to a spectacular cantilevered lookout with a see-through deck that is definitely not for the faint-hearted.

The Fitzroy Falls first became a public reserve in 1882 when the government set aside 4000 acres as a recreation area. The reserve attracted many day trippers, who journeyed in buggies, four-in-hands and carriages over a rough track from Moss Vale. For the more adventurous, a series of wooden ladders made a descent from the clifftop to the valley floor possible. Calls were made to establish the area as a national park as early as the 1890s, but it was to be 50 years before this dream became a reality. Mark Morton, after whom the park is named, was the local member of parliament for many years and it was through his energy and enthusiasm for the preservation of the natural environment that the park was gazetted in 1938.

Fitzroy Falls Reservoir

Fitzroy Falls Reservoir canal

MITTAGONG

& DISTRICT

MITTAGONG
& DISTRICT

Previous page:
Mittagong township
from Mt Gibraltar
and (opposite) an
example of a 19th
century building in
Mittagong

Approaching Mittagong from the north is a pleasant experience at any time of the year, particularly in autumn when the mature deciduous trees that line the wide entrance to the town show off their colour in all their splendid variety. Having arrived in Mittagong, the first thing to do is to take a deep breath of one of the Highlands most precious assets – the crisp, clean air. And then, visit the Southern Highlands Visitor Centre amidst its lovely gardens, where the richness and diversity of Highland life is showcased.

An Aboriginal word, Mittagong is said to mean "a place of native dogs". The name featured early in the European history of the Southern Highlands, first mentioned in 1816 when a survey team passed through the area. The first settlers came as early as 1821, occupying the flats at the foot of the Mittagong Range on the Old South Road a little to the east of the present town. It was not until the mid-1830s when the Great South Road

was constructed that Mittagong as we know it today began. Nestled on the northern side of Mt Gibraltar, locals think their town is "an overcoat warmer" than Bowral, just five kilometres away. In spring, the gardens of Mittagong bloom a little earlier than their southern neighbours and the winter frosts seem just that bit lighter.

Many generations of Frensham schoolgirls may disagree. For them the word Mittagong brings back memories of long train journeys and freezing mornings they would prefer to forget. But their school, Frensham, holds a special place in their hearts, for this is where they learned so many of the lessons of life, including how to survive a Highland winter!

With high ideals and firm views about the education of young women, Winifred West and Phyllis Clubbe opened their boarding school for girls in leased premises in 1913 with three pupils and five teachers. Frensham School, named for Miss West's birthplace in England, grew from these modest beginnings.

Frensham and its companion Sturt Workshops, begun by Miss West in 1941, have over the years become magnets for many talented teachers and artisans. Students from the various courses offered at Sturt produce work of the highest standard. Set in serene and beautiful gardens, Sturt enjoys an enviable reputation

as a fine contemporary art and craft gallery and is a wonderful place to enjoy lunch in the smart cafe.

Mittagong was home to another educational establishment that in its day educated the sons of many leading families, including the Throsbys, Osbornes, Badgerys and Tooths. Oaklands, a boarding school for boys run by the Oxford-educated Henry Southey, opened in 1875 in a building that for the previous 40 years had been run as the Fitzroy Inn. A Mittagong landmark, the building has recently been restored and once more welcomes guests. Some 15 inns and hotels operated in Mittagong at various times and happily a number of them survive, including the attractive Prince Albert Inn built in 1846 at Braemar, now the Poplars Restaurant, and somewhat later, the Prince of Wales Hotel, now Minniken Lodge.

The Maltings, a late 19th century industrial site, dominates a large area adjacent to the Fitzroy Inn and the railway line. Built in 1899 to process barley for the brewing industry, the complex eventually comprised three malt houses that together produced thousands of tonnes of barley malt each year. The cool Highland climate was ideal and with water supplied from the Nattai River that ran through the property, the venture, owned by brewers Tooth & Co from 1902, was highly successful. Its closure some 20 years ago has left this fine example of industrial architecture in limbo.

Not far up the hill behind the Fitzroy Inn is another house of considerable historical significance. Originally part of the Oaklands property, *The Hill* was home to Australia's first Prime Minister, Sir Edmund Barton, in 1887 and 1888. Barton brought his family to the Highlands in the hope that the clean air would help his asthmatic son. The two eldest sons attended Southey's school and Barton commuted by train to Sydney during the week. The house is also architecturally interesting as the only substantial house in the Southern Highlands to be built of pisé, a rammed-earth technique more often seen in dry climates.

Mittagong's streetscape, perhaps more than any of the major Southern Highlands towns, has retained much of its late-19th century character. Many fine buildings from the 1880s and 1890s survive, including the former office of the

The Maltings

Mittagong War Memorial and (right) Mittagong Antiques Centre

Commercial Banking Company of Sydney. Very much the "country bank", the company gave many NSW country towns their most impressive building and Mittagong's town centre is no exception. A handsome group of shops built by Mittagong mayor John Mealing in 1890 once housed the ES&A Bank and although the building has lost its iron lacework, it remains a dominant feature on Main Street. Opposite the Mealing Building is the lovely sandstone church of St Stephen, designed by ecclesiastical architect Edmund Blacket in 1876 and built on land given by the Fitzroy Iron Company.

The company was also indirectly responsible for the establishment of the town's most popular beauty spot. Lake Alexandra, surrounded by acres of parkland and bush, began its life as a water supply dam for the steam engines that hauled coal to the nearby iron works. The area was acquired by the local council in 1898 after the closure of the works and soon became a popular place for swimming, boating and picnicking, those leisure activities so beloved of the late Victorians. Lake Alexandra today is still a peaceful haven, a place to enjoy a leisurely walk, unpack a picnic hamper or feed the ducks.

In the charming residential area that surrounds Lake Alexandra are many stone and weatherboard cottages that have long since celebrated their centenary year. Some are decorated with the distinctive cast-iron lace manufactured in Mittagong at William Brazenall's Nattai Foundry. Brazenall was the last to commercially exploit the body of iron ore that runs behind Mittagong, something that entrepreneurs had tried to do, with mixed success, since 1848 when the first iron smelter in Australia began at the Fitzroy Iron Works.

The deposit of iron ore at Mittagong was discovered in 1833 when Major Thomas Mitchell's Great South Road was being constructed. It was to be another 15 years before a group of investors built a small blast furnace that in its first few years produced some good quality iron, but little profit. The Governor of NSW Sir Charles FitzRoy visited the works in 1850 and it was for

A garden sculpture at Sturt Craft Centre

The gardens at Frensham school

this occasion that 50 small figures of a lion rampant were cast as souvenir presentations. The few lions that have survived the years are now highly prized collectables and the stylised lion has become Mittagong's emblem. It features on the town signs, the street furniture and on the decorative banners that adorn the town centre.

Today, the site of Australia's first tentative steps towards establishing an iron industry is an open reserve and playing field where little evidence is visible of the substantial furnaces and rolling mills that once stood there. A commemorative plaque records the facts, but hardly conveys the significance of what took place, not just in terms of the genesis of the iron and steel industry, but also as the catalyst for the establishment and growth of New Sheffield, the company township that formed the nucleus of present day Mittagong. When the blast furnaces were finally demolished in 1911, the sandstone blocks were carted up the hill and used to build the Mittagong Memorial Hall which itself has recently been reborn as the Mittagong Playhouse. Everything from concerts and recitals to plays, workshops and seminars are hosted in the Highlands newest cultural centre.

Another legacy of the "iron age" in Mittagong is the imaginative street naming pattern in the 1884 subdivision of iron works land. Whoever was responsible for the names was a person of some education and wit, who used an obvious knowledge of science and technology to underscore the industrial origins of the town. Some 18 streets in Mittagong bear the names of prominent scientists, inventors, geologists, physicists and chemists of the 18th and 19th centuries. Bessemer Street, which runs along the northern boundary of the iron works site is perhaps the most obvious. Henry Bessemer invented a process of converting iron to steel and opened his own steel mills in Sheffield in the mid-19th century.

Others whose names are remembered in Mittagong are Siemens, Lyell, Murchison, Cavendish, Davey, Dalton, Priestley, Faraday, Owen, Huxley, Roscoe, Frankland, Henderson, Brewster, Tyndall and Spencer – all men and all British, a not surprising reflection of contemporary mores. Last but by no means least is Etheridge Street, named for Robert Etheridge, the only one of the 18 to have a real link with Mittagong. Largely forgotten today, in his time he was a well-known palaeontologist and curator of the Australian Museum for many years. Etheridge died in Mittagong in 1920.

Among the many attractions of Mittagong is the Antiques Centre, where more than 45 dealers show off their wares in a building that is itself 120 years old. Furniture, china and glass, artworks and collectables are displayed with great style.

Mittagong is also the starting point for one of the most scenic tourist drives in the Highlands – the long and winding road to Wombeyan Caves. Travelling first through open countryside to High Range the road passes through the impressive Bullio Tunnel before it begins the steep descent to the Wollondilly River at Goodmans Ford. The road and the five metre wide tunnel cut through solid rock were completed in 1899 and opened with great fanfare in January 1900. Built specifically as a tourist road to the caves, it had been the dream of many local business people for years and after much lobbying, the NSW government agreed to fund the construction. Still unsealed and narrow, the road has changed little over the years, but the slow trip is well worth the effort both for the splendid scenery along the way and the tremendously impressive Wombeyan Caves at journey's end.

Since a new by-pass section of the Hume Highway was constructed to the west of Mittagong about 10 years ago, taking thousands of cars and heavy vehicles out of the main street each day, the town has experienced something of a renaissance. Major streetscape improvements have made Mittagong an even more delightful place than before, which in turn has attracted more businesses, including several excellent restaurants, and people to explore and shop in the relaxed atmosphere of this pleasant country town – the gateway to the Southern Highlands.

A mosaic at Mittagong… vineyard from the air

Rural Mittagong

Winter scene Mittagong

View from Wanganderry on the Wombeyan Caves Road

Sheds at Wanganderry, a typical Australian property

On the Wombeyan Caves Road and (opposite) Bullio Tunnel

*Serenity ... the
Wollondilly River*

Goodmans Ford on the Wollondilly (left)
and dew drops hang in river-side trees

Derelict miners' cottages on Carrington Row and (opposite) ruined retorts, Joadja Creek

Hidden in an isolated valley not far west of Mittagong is the ghost town of Joadja Creek. The narrow access road winds through the bush until, suddenly, the valley floor widens and the extensive ruins of this once booming mining village spread out before you. As improbable as it seems today, this quiet and peaceful valley once echoed with the noise of a large industrial complex and the activity generated by a population that at one time numbered more than 1200.

Joadja Creek was established by the Australian Kerosene Oil & Mineral Company in the late 1870s to exploit the rich deposits of shale oil and coal in the valley. Over a 30 year period the operation produced kerosene, soap, candles and other by-products of the refining process for both the local and overseas market. Joadja became a unique, self-contained community, peopled largely by miners brought to Australia from Scotland by the AKO Company to overcome the shortage of skilled local labour.

The company provided housing for the miners and their families as well as a general store, post office, bakery and school. Farms on the ridges above Joadja Creek supplied vegetables, milk, butter and cheese, making the township almost self sufficient. Many varieties of fruit trees, some 7000 of them, were planted in the sheltered valley which in season produced an average of 100 cases of fresh fruit daily for the Sydney and export markets.

About three-quarters of the miners were Scottish, many of whom were experienced in the shale mining industry in their homeland. They brought to the area their distinctive dress, customs and accents and after the operation at Joadja ceased some decided to stay. Many Southern Highlanders proudly claim a family link to the stoic Scots who came half way around the world to work in the wild and beautiful Joadja Valley.

Inevitably, many never left Joadja. Accidents and a lack of adequate medical treatment took their toll and in the little cemetery on a hillside well away from the town are scattered headstones recording the final resting place of some of the 150 men, women and children who died there. Interestingly, the isolation of Joadja seems to have had the positive effect of protecting its inhabitants from outbreaks of epidemics such as whooping cough and diphtheria that often led to high infant mortality.

A century ago, the mining operation at Joadja was reaching the end of its relatively short life. Time, the ravages of bushfires, treasure hunters and neglect have all contributed to the gradual decline of this unique archaeological site. Today, whether exploring the ruins of the huge retorts or walking down Carrington Row, a street once lined with tiny brick houses, there is a tangible presence in the air. With eyes closed one can almost hear the ghosts of Joadja.

Old cottage in Richards Lane near Joadja Creek

Morning, Old South Road

BERRIMA
& DISTRICT

BERRIMA
& DISTRICT

B errima is one of the most important and interesting early colonial townships in NSW, but it offers much more to tourists than a window to the past. Berrima is a living village with an array of shops and galleries to please the most discerning buyer and cafes and restaurants offering everything from an ice cream to fine dining. On any weekend, this delightful village is crowded with people enjoying its special charm and atmosphere, much of which is the result of the generosity and breadth of early colonial town planning.

Major Thomas Mitchell, the Surveyor General of NSW, chose the site for Berrima in 1830 when he surveyed a line for his Great South Road. The beauty of the setting next to a reliable source of water in the Wingecarribee River and the boom in pastoral and agricultural activity in the district led Mitchell to envisage Berrima as the prosperous capital of the County of Camden, the antipodean equivalent of the English county town. Surveyor Robert Hoddle prepared a town plan based on this model, with a central market place overlooked by the site for the Church of England on the hill. As if to reinforce the power of Church and State, a gaol and court house were planned, of a size and style that befitted a county capital, to sit imposingly on the high ground to the north.

The first town lots in Berrima were sold in 1834, many of them to publicans or would-be innkeepers who snapped

Previous page: Aerial view of Berrima looking north and (right) shopping in Berrima, looking north towards the Surveyor General Inn and gaol

up the land around the market square in anticipation of brisk trade once the new road to the south was opened. Bryan McMahon's Berrima Inn was the first licensed hostelry in the township, soon followed by James Harper's Surveyor General, the Mail Coach, the Crown and Victoria Inns, to name but a few of 14 public houses that were once dotted around the town.

Berrima developed slowly at first, but by the late 1830s boom times were just around the corner. When the civil and military establishments at Bong Bong, site of the first settlement in the Highlands, were transferred to Berrima, the town seemed to be on the way to fulfilling its role as the commercial and administrative centre of the district. The impressive Berrima Court House was completed in 1838 and the gaol in 1839. Sandstone barracks to accommodate the military were built on a site overlooking the market

Harper's Mansion and Breens Restaurant formerly the Commercial Hotel

place and on the southern side of the Wingecarribee River stood the convict stockade that housed the gangs working on the construction and maintenance of the Great South Road.

Convict labour was also used to build the Berrima Gaol between 1836 and 1839. The original plan for the prison incorporated many of the new ideas of British prison reformers, who advocated separation and classification of inmates, and the introduction of constant surveillance. During its first 25 years, Berrima Gaol was used primarily as a lock-up, with a prison population of about 40. At times it was empty or occupied only by police and the lock-up keeper, but in the 1860s, it was extended and developed as a "model prison", where prisoners were kept in solitary confinement for

part of their sentence as a matter of course. Over the next 30 years, the Berrima Gaol gained an infamous reputation as one of the hardest places to do time.

By 1841, the town population numbered 249, bolstered by the passing parade of travellers and bullockies who drove the wagons and drays carrying wool, timber and grain to and from Sydney and the southern pastoral districts. The Great South Road had become a busy thoroughfare, with one visitor in 1842 noting that he had passed 90 loaded wagons between Campbelltown and Berrima.

Berrima experienced another boom period during the 1850s after the discovery of gold. A constant stream of hopefuls on their way to the diggings passed through the town, leaving plenty of money behind them in the public houses and stores. But within a few short years, the boom turned to bust when the Great Southern Railway bypassed Berrima in 1867, leading instead to the development of Mittagong, Bowral and Moss Vale. Over the next 40 years, Berrima drifted into a peaceful slumber. The Court House closed when sittings were transferred to Goulburn, business slowed to a trickle and house prices fell dramatically. In hindsight, we can be thankful that this was the case, for the very fact that Berrima became such a backwater ensured the survival of so much of its original Georgian architecture, making it one of the most intact townships of its type in NSW. More than 60 items of significance in Berrima are listed on the State Heritage Inventory, underlining the importance of the town as a largely intact 19th century settlement.

Much of the storytelling about Berrima has focused on its fascinating colonial past, but just as interesting is a period in its history during World War I, when the town became home for several hundred German enemy aliens and prisoners-of-war. Berrima Gaol had finally closed in 1909, but at the outbreak of war the dilapidated edifice was considered an ideal place to house some of the many German and Austrian civilians and mariners who were captive in Australia. The gaol was renovated, renamed the German

"The Hanover"   Berrima River (No 16)   B. Speer Photo

Internees Karl Wirthgren and Paul Wienicke in their yacht "Hanover" modelled on the Kaiser's "Hohenzollern"

Concentration Camp Berrima and in 1915 began receiving internees.

It is hard to imagine the culture shock that both the residents of Berrima and prisoners alike must have felt. On the one hand, the locals were suspicious of an enemy that propaganda had taught them to fear. For the internees, many of whom were more accustomed to the finer things of life, confinement in a somewhat tumble-down village of fewer than 100 people was a far cry from the sophistication of Europe. But the result, perhaps a surprise to everyone, was a unique success – an internment camp where guards, prisoners and local residents lived and worked together amicably.

Confined to their barracks between dusk and dawn, prisoners were free to roam by day within two miles of the gaol. They soon set about making the best of their detention and began to construct rustic huts along the banks of the Wingecarribee River for daytime recreation. Remarkable boats of all shapes and sizes, built as models of warships, submarines, sailing ships and even a floating Zeppelin, were constructed by the men from whatever materials they could lay their hands on. Their

enthusiasm seemed to know no bounds, with activities ranging from sports to vegetable gardening, music, woodcarving and language classes. They formed an orchestra and a theatrical group, performing both for their fellow internees and the local residents.

Berrima experienced its first taste of tourism as word spread about the activities of "The Germans". Visitors came from near and far to the regattas on the river and the sports days. The village derived significant economic benefits over the 4½ years the camp operated, but in August, 1919, it all came to an end when the pris-oners marched out of Berrima to the station at Moss Vale to begin their journey home. The town went back to sleep and nearly 50 years would pass before it would awake to a new tourist boom.

Increasing awareness during the 1960s of the value of our colonial heritage led to the classification of the town of Berrima by the National Trust in 1974. Many of the decaying historic buildings were restored and reopened as restaurants, galleries, antique and craft shops. The Surveyor General Inn, claiming the status of being the oldest continuously licensed hotel in

White Horse Inn and Berrima House where, according to folklore, bushranger Ben Hall once slept on the verandah

Holy Trinity Church, Berrima designed by Edmund Blacket and completed in 1849

Australia, was always a tourist drawcard for the town, but gradually as other old inns were brought back to life, visitors came for more than just a passing look at the town's faded beauty.

The Crown Inn, built by William Taylor in 1845, was one of the first buildings to be restored, opening as a fine art and craft gallery, Berrima Galleries, in 1968. On the other side of the road, Breen's Commercial Hotel, after years as a private home and boarding house, became the Colonial Inn Restaurant, now called Breens. Similarly, the Victoria Inn and its associated outbuildings have been lovingly restored and for many years welcomed guests to its restaurant. Built by Jewish ex-convict Joseph Levy in 1840, the inn is one of the best examples of colonial Georgian architecture in Berrima. One of a group of enterprising merchants in Berrima in its early years, Levy also operated the Imperial Brewery on the site, producing "the best colonial beer, equal to any in the colony".

Publican James Harper of the Surveyor General Inn also prospered and his house is another fine survivor from the 1830s. Commanding a view over the whole of the township, Harper's Mansion, like most of the buildings in Berrima, has had a variety of uses during its long history. Sold in 1853 to the Catholic church, it was used as the Presbytery for St Scholastica's Catholic Church (now St Francis Xavier) until the late 1890s, after which it was occupied by the sisters of Our Lady of the Sacred Heart, who ran a school in Berrima before they moved over the hill to Bowral. After years of neglect, the National Trust of Australia acquired Harper's Mansion and restored the derelict property. Now leased as a private residence, lights shine once more from the windows of the house on Harper's Hill.

Design detail of St Francis Xavier Church, Berrima,
much favoured by architect Augustus Pugin

At the other end of the village, like twin sentinels, the Anglican and Catholic churches sit atop the rises of the north and south banks of the Wingecarribee River. Both built in the Gothic Revival style, each has impressive architectural credentials. Holy Trinity Anglican Church was designed by the prolific ecclesiastical architect, Edmund Blacket. Completed in 1849, this delightful building was constructed from the warm yellow sandstone quarried on the site. Said to be the first church of his own design completed in Australia, Blacket used as his model the parish church of St Peter in Biddestone, Wiltshire, complete with its distinctive bellcote. Ironically perhaps, the original in England was long ago demolished.

The strong architectural link between Australia and Britain is no better demonstrated than in the Catholic church of St Francis Xavier on the southern side of the river. Built to a design of Augustus Pugin, the noted pioneer of the Gothic Revival movement in 19th century England, the church is a unique example of the architect's work, reflecting his exacting standards of proportion. Unaltered since its completion in 1851, it is the only Pugin church left structurally intact either in NSW or England, making it a heritage item of great significance.

In recent years Berrima has experienced tremendous growth in tourism. But success is a double-edged sword and the momentum created by cultural tourism has put pressure on the very qualities that make Berrima unique. On the positive side, the bypassing of Berrima by a freeway in the mid-1980s, unlike the 1867 railway bypass, has led to its revitalisation as a residential village of great charm and beauty, not to mention the pleasure of wandering the streets untroubled by a constant stream of traffic on the "Great South Road", the Hume Highway. Berrima has never been more prosperous than it is today, both as a tourist destination and a sought after place to live. A leisurely walk through the village is a step back in time, with vivid reminders at every turn of the rich history of this very special town.

Berrima Galleries (above), Old Bakery Cottage and (opposite) Berrima General Store

*S*tanding on the high ground of the township, both in the literal and moral sense, the Court House is undoubtedly the most impressive building in Berrima. Completed in 1838, it was visible from all over the town. At that time the walls of Berrima Gaol were set back some 20 metres from where they are today. Another 50 years would pass before the governor's residence and other staff accommodation were constructed in front of the gaol, so obstructing the vista to and from the Court House that was so much a part of the early town plan for Berrima. Mortimer Lewis, the architect for the building, was the leading exponent of the Greek Revival style in Australia and of the many court houses he designed during his tenure as Colonial Architect, Berrima is among the best. Following a basic formula, with a clerestory-lit court room flanked by lower wings that housed the offices, the design was similar to numerous court buildings erected in England during the post-Waterloo period. At Berrima, the central high court room section was carried forward in the form of a giant portico and Lewis specified elegant columns of the Tuscan order rather than the more usual fluted Greek Doric design. The design and siting of the Berrima Court House would have sent a clear message to the populace of the power and majesty of the law.

Used for Courts of Quarter Sessions from 1838 and for the Supreme Court circuit from 1841, Berrima Court House was the scene of many memorable trials. Bushranger William "Jackey Jackey" Westwood was the first to be tried at a Supreme Court sitting in Berrima and was sentenced to transportation to Tasmania by Judge Alfred Stephen, later Chief Justice of NSW. Local magistrates dealt with the more mundane aspects of the legal system such as the issuing of inn licences, assignment of convicts and the settlement of minor cases.

As courts were established in other towns in the district, the activities of the District Court at Berrima were wound down and in 1884, Berrima Court House was finally closed. For the next 40 years it was used as a meeting and concert hall, a School of Arts and during World War I, to accommodate German prisoners of war,

becoming steadily more dilapidated. The threat of demolition in the late 1920s was vetoed and so today the building remains a focal point in the village of Berrima. A restoration project completed in 1976 by the NSW Department of Public Works brought the building back to near-original appearance and it now houses a museum focusing on the story of Berrima and the legal system in colonial NSW.

Gaol (above) and at left the Berrima Court House

Wingecarribee River at Berrima and Riverview Cottage
(above) which once housed a school for young ladies

Berrima's fine 19th century sandstone and brick architecture is justifiably celebrated, but the simple slab and bark houses of the ordinary folk are less renowned. By their very nature, few of these structures have survived the passage of time and the ravages of bushfires. A notable exception is to be found on the southern fringe of the village, where an 1880s slab cottage, "The Gunyah", has recently had new life breathed into its tiny rooms.

This simple house was the first Australian home for German immigrants Adolph and Sophia Barth who arrived in Australia in 1880 and immediately came to Berrima where Sophia's brother, Robert Metz, was in business as a stonemason. They soon acquired land and set about building a new home of vertical timber slabs and bush timbers, very much in the Australian vernacular style. Distinguished by a wide sandstone verandah on two sides, probably courtesy of the expertise of Robert Metz, the cottage originally had only three rooms – a parlour and two bedrooms – with the usual detached kitchen at the rear.

Unoccupied for many years, the house was in danger of collapse when the present owner purchased it and began the task of making it habitable once more. Taking a conservative approach to the restoration, the original fabric of the building and many of the internal features have been retained in their original state, giving a feeling of authenticity both inside and out.

The Gunyah at Berrima

Left: Horses at water near Berrima and (above) trees beside the Old Hume Highway at Berrima, part of the Remembrance Drive between Sydney and Canberra that commemorates Australians who died in World War II

Medway Road at Berrima and (below) geese on Minnows Drive

Medway Road,
Berrima

HOUSES
& GARDENS

HOUSES
& GARDENS

One thing that epitomises the Southern Highlands is its gardens. From the formal and elegant to woodland dells, from exuberant cottage gardens to country gardens in the landscape style, some of the finest cool climate gardens and the most passionate and accomplished gardeners are to be found in the Highlands.

The enthusiasm for gardens and gardening has a long history in the area and is very directly linked to creating a setting for the many grand country houses built in the latter years of the 19th century and early 20th century. Characterised today by extensive exotic tree plantings that in their maturity give the Highlands its distinctive look, the local environment is one that has been greatly altered by human hands. More than a century ago, the fine houses of Burradoo, Moss Vale and Sutton Forest stood stark and exposed in bare paddocks. We must thank the gardeners of these early days for the beauty and abundance we enjoy today, for they built the framework and fostered the culture of gardening that is still so strong

A number of families of wealth and influence have left their mark on the Southern Highlands, but perhaps none more so than the Horderns. Three of the best known houses in Bowral were once owned by members of that great retailing dynasty – *Retford Park*, *Hopewood*

and *Milton Park*. Brothers Sam, Anthony and Lebbeus Hordern were a glamourous trio who could afford to live extravagantly and indulge their shared passion for motor cars and stock breeding. But they also surrounded their properties with gardens of great beauty and one of them, *Milton Park*, is now considered one of the great gardens of the world.

Anthony Hordern purchased the 1200 acre property in 1910 and after building a large country house designed by Sydney architects Morrow and de Putron, began the task of developing the garden on the exposed hilltop site. Supervised by his first wife Viola, the garden was originally of more formal Edwardian design. After her death in 1929, Tony Hordern married Ursula Mary Bullmore who, with great flair, changed the garden during the 1930s to one of grand expanses of lawn, sloping terraces, walkways, pools and secret corners. Mary Hordern was a bold gardener, unafraid of moving advanced plants around until she was quite happy with their position. Today we can enjoy the brilliance of her deft eye for design, colour and proportion. This is a garden that delights the senses in each season

Near *Milton Park* is *Retford Park*, the two storey Italianate house built in 1888 by Samuel Hordern and inherited by his son Samuel II in 1909. Lady Hordern was a passionate gardener and planted a vast array of

*Previous page:
Historic Oldbury
from the air and
(right) Milton Park*

flower beds, a formal rose garden, vegetable garden and orchard that supplied enough cut flowers and produce to supply both *Retford Park* and the Horderns' Sydney home in Darling Point.

The third of the Hordern brothers, Lebbeus, bought *Hopewood* in 1912 and immediately made additions to the house and built the dairy and horse pavilion. He was also avidly interested in the garden and during his ownership *Hopewood* became a showpiece. Many of the old trees in the garden were planted during Lebbeus Hordern's tenure which came to an end after his death in 1929. After many years, new owners are now restoring the house and garden

Another hillside property that has been transformed by its garden is *Whitley* at Sutton Forest. Supreme Court judge Sir William Owen built the house on land subdivided from the original 1820s *Oldbury* property. Completed in about 1890, the Tudor style house sat incongruously in the middle of a treeless paddock. Judge Owen, his son Sir Langer Owen and the property's next owner, Thomas Heney, editor of *The Sydney Morning Herald*, were responsible for the early tree planting, including many oaks and elms and the distinctive hawthorn hedge that surrounds the property. The present owners bought *Whitley* in 1980 and have sensitively restored the house, cottages and stable. One of the most striking features of the property is the layered hawthorn hedge that surrounds it. Over the winters of 1984 and 1985, a professional hedge layer, seven times champion of England, came to *Whitley* and tamed the rampant hawthorn to create the impressive hedge that now lines both sides of Oldbury Road.

Building on the framework of wonderful old trees, the garden we see today has evolved over the past 20 years. As well as the formal elegance of the rose garden planted with rugosa roses, there is a nut orchard of walnut, pecan, hazelnut and Spanish chestnut and extensive native plantings of eucalypt, acacia, telopea, banksia and melaleuca.

In 1942 *Kennerton Green* was a fibro cottage on five acres with two trees, a privet hedge, rangy black wattles

and a few pine trees. Now almost 60 years later, this Mittagong property is one of the most beautiful gardens in Australia and welcomes more visitors than any of the private gardens in the Highlands.

When Ivan "Snow" Hansen started to clear the privet for his employer and owner of the property, Percy Rowe, it was a slow process and it was not until 1954 that the first of many trees that were to be planted over the next 12 years found their way into the garden. After Mr Rowe's death in 1966, *Kennerton Green* passed to his

nephew, Sir John Pagan, and from this time on the garden really began to take shape. Sir John and his wife Marjorie renovated and extended the house and with "Snow" Hansen created a magnificent garden.

The present owner, who bought the property in 1988, is a passionate gardener whose inspiration comes from the traditions of England and Europe. While the original borders, huge wisterias, camellias and mature trees near the house have been preserved, the garden has been vastly extended, with a number of themed rooms flowing one from the other. This is not just a spring garden, but one that blooms over a long period

Dappled sunlight on a lane at Milton Park (opposite) and Oldbury, built about 1828 (above)

Whitley (top) and (below) detail of the "laid" hedge and (opposite) surrounded by exotic trees

from August onwards and by November, when the splendid collection of roses are at their best, *Kennerton Green* is probably at its most beautiful.

Buskers End at Bowral is the creation of skilled garden designer Joan Arnold who bought the property in 1976. Overgrown by weeds and invading bush, and exposed to the harsh weather from the south-west, the garden had little to recommend it except its beautiful trees. Once windbreaks were planted, the labour of love to establish this garden of rare and interesting plants began. This is a gardener's garden, where rare and unusual plants and trees form part of the spectacular displays of massed bulbs in spring and colourful perennial borders in summer.

Both at *Buskers End* and *Kennerton Green*, the focus of attention is the garden. But at *Oldbury* in Sutton Forest, the reverse is true. Delightful as the garden is, it is a foil for the lovely sandstone farmhouse built by James Atkinson in about 1828. Atkinson came from the village of Oldbury on the Medway River in Kent, England, and when he received his land grant in 1821 he not only named his property for his former home, but the small creek that ran through it became the Medway Rivulet. The house he built also reflected his Kentish origins, for it is very much in the English farmhouse style and quite unlike most of the early country houses in NSW. Simple and unpretentious, the character of *Oldbury* is somewhat like that of its builder, a fine man who was universally admired for his kindness and practical good sense. The two storey house with a simple portico entrance is beautifully sited at the foot of Mt. Gingenbullen and framed by some wonderful trees.

The house and two detached outbuildings, the dairy and kitchen, were sensitively restored some 20 years ago, with simple but effective landscaping. Numerous old elm trees along Oldbury Creek are said to have been planted by Atkinson, but the present garden is a recent and welcome development. The house and garden have probably never looked better than they do today with manicured lawns, neatly trimmed hedges and wide sweeping gravel driveway leading the eye to this most

Buskers End
in winter

New architecture sits comfortably with the old on the slopes of Mt Gibraltar

charming and important of the early colonial houses in the Southern Highlands.

Newbury is another of the early Sutton Forest properties of great historical significance. Granted in 1822 to Captain John Nicholson, Harbourmaster of Sydney, it is said that when he found that James Atkinson's property was to be called *Oldbury*, he decided that his should be *Newbury*! For some years Captain Nicholson was an absentee landowner, but he moved permanently to Sutton Forest in 1842, becoming one of the leading citizens in the district. For 15 years he was the District

Throsby Park, built by Charles Throsby II in 1834 to accommodate his growing family. He and his wife Betsy had 17 children

Coroner and served as a magistrate for 20 years. But his most enduring if least known contribution to civic life was his design of 1831 for what became the unofficial Australian flag for more than 70 years. The Federation flag as it became known is now flying again in Sutton Forest, not far from *Newbury* and the cemetery of All Saints Church where Captain Nicholson is buried.

The gardens of the Southern Highlands are highly diverse and while the larger estates with their historic homes are the best known, there are also many smaller treasures of more recent creation. *Hillview* at Exeter is

one of those treasures, a garden that delights dedicated plantspeople as much as it does the amateur gardener. Here is a collection of rare bulbs and alpine plants collected by the owner over many years and several plant hunting trips to Europe, the Middle East and America. Since the late 1970s, the garden at *Hillview* has evolved from an almost bare one acre block with two Himalayan cedars to a "secret garden" of outstanding beauty and variety. The old weatherboard house once prominent on the hillside is no longer visible from the road, enfolded by the trees and shrubs that form the backdrop to the circular terrace gardens.

The long history of European settlement of the Southern Highlands and the nature of the people who have come to the district over the past 180 years has endowed the area with a rich and unbroken architectural heritage. Outstanding examples of every style of house from the early cottage to modern classics are found in the Highlands. Many have been carefully maintained over their long lives, others more recently renovated, restored or built, but by whatever means, the result is a remarkably large group of interesting and historic houses spread throughout the district.

Among the most important from the earliest days of settlement are those on the old properties such as *Browley* and *Oldbury* from the 1820s, *Throsby Park*, *Vine Lodge* and *Newbury* from the 1830s, *Comfort Hill* and *Eling Forest* from the 1840s. At Burradoo and in the major towns, many examples from the later Victorian period are hidden behind the hedges, from the almost impossibly ornate *Yean House* to the simple elegance of *Elvo* (now Oxley College). Into the 20th century, *Moidart* designed by architect Laidley Downing, *Greyleaves* designed by Professor Leslie Wilkinson, both in Burradoo, and *Invergowrie* at Exeter were all built in the 1930s and surrounded by marvellous gardens. Although the heyday of the great country estate may have passed, the Southern Highlands is still a place where houses of the best design and great style continue to be built and the fine gardens of the future created.

Red Cow Farm (top) and the Exeter Hillview

Parsley Cottage in Berrima (left) and (above) Prittlewell at Fitzroy Falls with (below) rhododendrons that bloom so prolifically in the Highlands

Mt Broughton (both pages), a country house built by the Kater family, is now a luxury hotel

Garden walk
at Moidart

Redlands, Mittagong

Retford Park,
one of three
country estates
originally owned by
members of the
Hordern family

A corner of the garden at Gowan Brae

The rose "Gowan Brae", grown by Heather Cant

Profusion of bulbs at Hillview, Exeter and (right) part of Moidart's formal garden

From the earliest days of the colony, successive governors of NSW chose to maintain a residence away from Sydney where they could occasionally escape the heat of summer and the busy round of vice-regal duties. Government House at Parramatta fulfilled this need for many years, but as the Southern Highlands gained fame as a healthy holiday resort where one could enjoy the cooler Highland climate and the pleasures of country living, attention turned to finding a suitable house.

The Earl of Belmore, Governor of NSW from 1867 to 1872, began the vice-regal association with Moss Vale when he leased Throsby Park as a country residence. His successor, Sir Hercules Robinson, also visited the Highlands from time to time, but it was not until 1882 that Sir Henry Parkes' NSW government purchased a property specifically for use as a vice-regal retreat. The house they bought for £6000 was "Prospect", the Sutton Forest home of Robert P. Richardson of Richardson and Wrench estate agents. Renamed "Hillview", the house was a silent witness to the comings and goings of some 16 State governors for the next 75 years

"Hillview" was soon deemed too small for its purpose and major renovations and extensions began almost immediately. A further £10,000 was spent to bring the house up to what was considered a suitable standard, expenditure that caused the Parkes' government considerable political embarrassment. When completed the house had 46 rooms, nine bathrooms and could accommodate about 50 people and a staff of up to 35.

Hillview before restoration (left) and the water tower, carriage house and stable (below)

By the late 1950s the house was being used for only a small part of the year and in 1958 the State government put "Hillview" up for auction. For the next 30 years it was the private residence of Mr Edwin Klein, who, in 1986, gifted the house to the NSW government, complete with most of the original furnishings.

Set on 150 acres, the house is perched atop a hillside and reached by a winding, elm-lined driveway more than a kilometre long. Surrounded by several acres of gardens, "Hillview" is a rambling house of a somewhat eccentric mixture of architectural styles. For the past 15 years, the property has been in mothballs but now, with strict guidelines in place to protect this heritage building, "Hillview" is undergoing extensive renovations to become an exclusive boutique hotel.

Bellbird at Goodmans Ford on the Wollondilly

A home at Robertson (below) with a view to the sea and (right) a modern pavilion style home in Berrima

A water garden at Gowan Brae

Daffodils in the snow

Forest Lodge at Alpine, once a Cobb & Co staging post

Apolima, Exeter

Random stone pathways meander through cottage gardens

Part of the garden at Prittlewell, Fitzroy Falls

Kennerton Green, the Highlands most visited garden

Redlands, Mittagong (left) and Kennerton Green

ON THE
LAND

ON THE
LAND

The substantially urbanised area along the main arterial road running between Mittagong, Bowral and Moss Vale gives little hint of the many grazing, agricultural and horticultural enterprises, both new and old, that thrive in the Highlands. As suburban gardens give way to rolling green hills you are suddenly aware of heading into real farming territory and in the picturesque countryside to the east of Bowral are some of the most productive properties in the Southern Highlands. The road to Kangaloon meanders through the lush pastures of dairy farms and climbs high above the Wingecarribee Reservoir where the views over the water and the Wingecarribee Swamp are spectacular.

It is hard to imagine now that the whole of this rich and fertile belt of land was once covered by almost impenetrable forest, known to the early settlers as the Yarrawa Brush. In the red soil of this basalt country grew gigantic stands of gum and messmate, some of which had trunks that stretched for nearly 30 metres to the first branch and were up to 15 metres in circumference. Intertwined with the trees, ferns, cabbage palms and sassafras were tough vines and creepers. But after the passage of the Robertson Land Acts of 1861, the prospect of owning a piece of this rich land brought settlers up the escarpment from Kiama and Jamberoo and the process of clearing the brush began.

Previous page:
Alpacas at
Coolaroo and
bagging potatoes at
Wildes Meadow

By 1865, selectors had taken up some 30,000 acres of land and slowly the small villages of Robertson, Burrawang, Wildes Meadow and Kangaloon formed. The most progressive of these hamlets at that time was Burrawang, described as "a singularly energetic place" with both a post office and Church of England school attended by as many as 70 pupils. By 1871, three licensed hotels, the Sassafras, the Prince Alfred and Cliffords, were helping quench the thirsts of the hard working locals. Burrawang today is home to a wide cross section of people, with descendants of the original settlers now sharing the village with weekend visitors and escapees from city life. The farmers have been joined by an enthusiastic and talented artistic community that regularly stages plays and entertainments in the refurbished School of Arts. There is no doubt that Burrawang is one of the most appealing of the Highland villages.

Neighbouring Wildes Meadow is more a locale than a village these days, although it once had the trappings of a small town – a church, school, bank and hotel. The waters of the Fitzroy Falls Reservoir are visible from many vantage points in Wildes Meadow and, surrounded by green hills that fold one into another, this is an area of truly beautiful scenery. The Belmore Falls Road to Robertson cuts through the northern reaches of the Morton National Park and over the creek at the top of the lovely falls, named for the Earl of Belmore, the first governor of NSW to choose the Southern Highlands as a country retreat.

Poised on the ridge above Macquarie Pass National Park, Robertson is an essentially rural community that now caters for an ever increasing number of tourists and a growing permanent population. The idea of naming a town in honour of a politician would perhaps not find favour with today's somewhat jaundiced public, but that is just what the new selectors of the Yarrawa Brush did in 1865, so pleased were they with the Secretary for Lands, the Honourable John Robertson. It was to his Land Acts of 1861 that they attributed their good fortune in being able to purchase such rich and

Myra Vale Road,
Wildes Meadow

fertile land, and in response to a people's petition, the government of the day agreed to their request. And so the fledgling township of Robertson came into being.

Potatoes were among the first crops planted by the pioneer settlers, not surprisingly given the Irish background of many of them. There are few lovelier sights than to see neatly ploughed and seeded red soil paddocks in contrast to the emerald green pastures that surround them. Still synonymous with Robertson, a sack of freshly dug "apples of the earth" is a most highly regarded local commodity, even though production today is not nearly as great as it was even 10 years ago.

But the humble potato is bringing worldwide recognition to the Highlands through the success of a highly innovative research project. With its head office in Moss Vale, a local company has developed a revolutionary new way of producing miniature seed potatoes, cheaper, faster and in greater volume than anyone else in the world. So secret is the technique that only a few people know the whole process. From production facilities in Australia, the United States, Mexico, China and India, the company sends seed potatoes all over the world, with french fries as the target market for the potatoes produced. Indirectly this locally based agricultural business is making sure that the Highlands remains famous for "spuds".

At the Robertson Show the potato race still draws a big crowd to watch strong men run with a full sack on their backs. A country show in the true sense of the word, the Agricultural and Horticultural Society has run the annual show on the same site since 1889. Among the members of the show committee are descendants of the first settlers in Robertson, many of whom still maintain family links with the land.

Traditionally, dairying has been a mainstay of the Southern Highlands rural scene. Dairy produce was probably the earliest export from the district, with the farmers of the 1820s sending small quantities of butter and cheese to Sydney. But the real boost to dairy production came when refrigeration and butter making machinery came into more general use in the 1870s.

Over many years, milk was sent by rail to Sydney and butter manufactured in small factories dotted throughout the district. Again, Robertson made a name for itself when the Robertson Cheese Factory opened in 1936 and during its first year won every first prize at the Dairy Produce Exhibition.

In the heyday of the dairy industry, there were more than 300 dairy farms in the Highlands milking some 11,000 cows. The rationalisation and deregulation of the dairy industry in recent years has resulted in many farmers going out of the industry, but those who remain are highly efficient and productive. Today, there are only about 5000 milking cows on just 26 dairy farms, most of which are in the Kangaloon area.

But as one door closes, inevitably another opens and in a sense this has always been the story of farming and grazing in the Highlands. For more than 50 years from the 1820s, wheat and other cereal crops such as rye and barley were the major crops grown, until rust attacked the wheat. In the golden years of the 1950s, sheep were widely grazed, but beef cattle and even small herds of alpacas have since taken their place to a large degree.

Over the past 15 years several primary industries new to the Highlands have developed, complementing the more traditional ways of living off the land. One of the most promising of these new industries is grape growing. Although vines were planted locally on the large estates in the 1820s, and at Mandemar in the 1860s by a family of German immigrants, the grapes were largely for domestic use. Modern wine production in the Southern Highlands began in 1983 with the Joadja Winery, followed in 1990 by Eling Forest Winery, established on a historic property just south of Berrima. Today, vineyards are being planted throughout the district in fields where cattle and sheep once grazed and boutique wineries are increasingly becoming an attraction for visitors. There are now about 45 vineyards in the area and a local vignerons' association that is working on the development of viticulture and recognition of the Southern Highlands as a distinct winemaking region.

Productive rich red soil on Myra Vale Road, Wildes Meadow

The climatic conditions and high altitude make the product of the area quite different from the more famous NSW grape growing regions of the Hunter Valley and Mudgee. Soils, wind and storm patterns vary markedly over even the smallest area producing micro-climates that make the grapes from each vineyard slightly different. A large number of grape varieties have been planted, including chardonnay, sauvignon blanc, shiraz, cabernet sauvignon, malbec and merlot and although it is a little too soon to say which will be the most successful, there is a great deal of confidence in the future of the local industry.

Olive groves are also springing up in many parts of the Highlands, particularly in the lower rainfall belt in the western area of the Wingecarribee Shire. This infant industry will take some time to develop, for it takes olive trees some six or seven years before they bear reliable fruit and in terms of commercial viability. Most groves in the Highlands are quite small, with an average of 300 to 400 trees. Again, as with the growing of wine grapes, these enterprises fall into the boutique category,

in most cases supplying high quality, hand picked fresh fruit or olives for brining.

The diversification of Southern Highlands primary producers is very much a reflection of changing markets, and the tastes of Australia and Australians. Fifty years ago, we consumed little wine and olives were mysterious things eaten by Italian and Greek Australians. Where once the Highlands grew exotic flower species for the Sydney floral trade, waratahs, banksias and other natives species are now fashionable and command high prices for premium export blooms.

The range of niche-market commodities grown and manufactured in the Highlands is impressive. As more and more people look at alternative or additional crops to replace or supplement farm income, the diversity of local rural production increases. Lavender, mustard seed, nut trees, organic vegetables and berries are just a few of the many products to be found on the farms of the Southern Highlands. The challenge for the future is to balance old and new to keep the farming tradition of the district firmly intact.

An olive grove at Wildes Meadow and (above) chestnut farm in the Werai district near Moss Vale

Lavender at Farmgate, Wildes Meadow

Exotic mushrooms are grown in a disused railway tunnel near Mittagong

Highland cattle at the Robertson Show

Robertson Show potato race

A Waler horse at Southern Star Waler Stud in
Robertson and (below) a black Angus

Cuties at the Robertson Show

Thoroughbred horses at Sutton Forest (left)
and sheep on Sheepwash Road

*One of the
numerous plant
nurseries in
Southern Highlands*

Apples at
Bowral market

A patchwork of crops at Robertson

INDEX

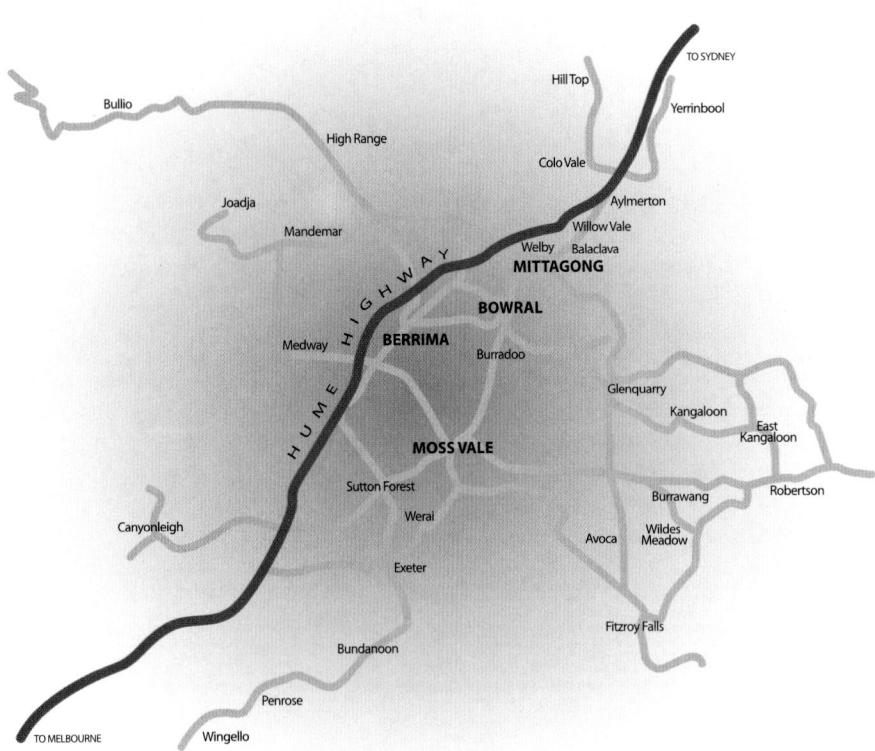

Bullio

High Range

Joadja

Mandemar

Medway

Canyonleigh

HUME HIGHWAY

Hill Top

TO SYDNEY

Yerrinbool

Colo Vale

Aylmerton

Willow Vale

Welby   Balaclava

MITTAGONG

BOWRAL

BERRIMA

Burradoo

Glenquarry

Kangaloon

East
Kangaloon

MOSS VALE

Sutton Forest

Werai

Avoca

Wildes
Meadow

Burrawang

Robertson

Exeter

Fitzroy Falls

Bundanoon

Penrose

Wingello

TO MELBOURNE

A Window To The Southern Highlands is a HIGH*Life* publication.
HIGH*Life* Magazine, about country life in the Southern Highlands of New South Wales,
is published six times a year and is available by subscription or at newsagents.
Telephone: 02 4861 6311